AF477242

Happiness is about being free, to become free you have to have courage to take the leap.

ENLIGHTENED PUBLISHING

Write who you want to become,
think about it and write in
great detail

What risk would you take if you knew you could not fail?

What is your greatest strength?
Have any of your recent actions
demonstrated this strength?

What are the top five things you cherish in your life?

How old would you be if you didn't know how old you are?

When do you stop calculating risk and rewards, and just do it?

At what time in your recent past
have you felt most passionate and
alive?

What do you most connect with? Why?

What one piece of advice would you offer a newborn child?

Which is worse, failing or never trying?

Why do we do things we dislike and like the things we never seem to do?

What are you avoiding?

What is the one job/cause/activity that could get you out of bed happily for the rest of your life? Are you doing it now?

When it's all said and done, will you have said more than you've done?

What are you most grateful for?

What would you say is one thing you'd like to change in the world?

Do you find yourself influencing your world, or it influencing you?

Are you doing what you believe in or settling for what you're doing?

What are you committed to?

Which worries you more, doing things right or doing the right things?

If joy became the national currency, what kind of work would make you wealthy?

Have you been the kind of friend you'd want as one?

Do any of the things that used to
upset you a few years ago matter
at all today? What's changed?

Would you rather have less work
to do or more work you enjoy doing?

What permission do you
need/want to move forward?

Really, what do you have to lose if you go for it?

How different would your life be if there weren't any criticism in the world?

We're always making choices. Are you choosing for your story or for someone else's?

What if this was the last time..?

If tomorrow was my last day, would I have any regrets?

What can I do today that can shape
my future in exciting ways?

What kind of impact do you want to have?

Last but not least,
live the life you want not the
life others tell you or expect
from you.
Society doesn't have a say in
how you decide to live your
life.
Be happy, make yourself
happy
in order to make others,
it doesn't work any other way.
There is more to life than
what we see and what we were
told.
It's up to us to find it!
Be happy, be you!

"Be a story worth telling!"

Know thyself. Socrates

"Keep your head clear. It doesn't matter how bright the path is if your head is always cloudy." ~Unknown